IN THE MEANTIME

WHAT TO DO WHEN THERE'S NOTHING YOU CAN DO

In The Meantime Participant's Guide

Cover design by North Point Media

Italics in Scripture quotations are the author's emphasis.

Unless otherwise indicated, Scripture quotations are from:
The Holy Bible, New International Version (NIV)

Printed in the United States of America

15 16 17 18 19 20 10 9 8 7 6 5 4 3 2 1

[CONTENTS]

[USING THE PARTICIPANT'S GUIDE]

[BEFORE SESSION 1]

1. Read through pages 9–10 to gain an overview of the study.

2. Read through the content in *Session 1* on pages 11–14.

3. Read through *A Typical Group Meeting* on page 7 to gain an understanding of the flow of this study.

[DURING EACH GROUP MEETING]

1. Turn to the *Notes* page, and watch the video segment.

2. Have a conversation using the *Discussion Questions* listed in the guide.

3. Read the *Think About It* section aloud.

4. Review the *Before the Next Session* homework at the close of the chapter.

LEADING THE DISCUSSION

If you find yourself as the lead facilitator of the *Discussion Questions,* here are three things to consider during your group meetings:

CULTIVATE DISCUSSION
It is the ideas of everyone in the group that make a group meeting successful. Your role as the leader is to create an environment in which people feel safe to share their thoughts.

STAY ON TRACK
While you want to leave space for group members to think through the discussion, make sure the conversation is contributing to the topic being discussed that session. Don't let it veer off on tangents. Go with the flow, but be ready to nudge the conversation in the right direction when necessary.

PRAY
This is the most important thing you can do as a leader and as a group. Pray that God is not only present at your group meetings, but that he is directing them.

[A TYPICAL GROUP MEETING]

Social Time	30 minutes
Video	20 minutes
Discussion	45 minutes
Prayer	15 minutes

[INTRODUCTION]

At some point in your life, you will face a set of circumstances beyond your control. You'll have a problem that can't be solved or a tension that can't be resolved. What do you do?

Sometimes it's a relational conflict. Maybe you're in a troubled marriage. Neither you nor your spouse wants a divorce, but you both resist changing your ways. The future of the relationship looks grim. Or maybe you're facing challenges with your children. You keep telling them that their grades matter and will be important in the future, but they won't listen. You're afraid they won't realize you're right until they're seniors in high school and their college options are limited.

Sometimes it's a money problem. Your financial dreams aren't coming true. They can't come true, and there's nothing you can do about it. Things didn't work out professionally. A downturn in the economy robbed you of time you can't recover. You've been wrongly accused of doing something you didn't do and bumped out of an industry. The problem is permanent. There is no solution.

Sometimes it's a health issue. Illness is your new reality—your new normal. It won't kill you, but it's debilitating and chronic. It will be with you for the rest of your life. There's a treatment, but no cure.

Whatever the specifics, we all face seasons that we'll call *in the meantime*. These are times when you're not looking for a solutions

. . . because your circumstances have no solution. You have options, but they're all bad. If you try to solve your problems, you'll only create more problems.

What do you do *in the meantime?* You can run, but you don't want to run. You can abandon your family, but you don't want to abandon your family. You can give up on your child, but you don't want to give up on your child. You can quit, but you don't want to quit. You can drink yourself into oblivion, but you know that's a temporary solution, and it'll only create bigger problems.

Worst of all, you sense that your problems are making you jealous and envious of other people. They seem to be living wrinkle-free lives, and you want that for yourself. It's hard not to feel angry and resentful. You hear Christians talk about how God answered their prayers, and you wonder why he seems to be ignoring yours. You've come to a place where it feels like there's no point in continuing. There's no point in battling. Maybe you don't see any point in living.

During the six sessions of this study, we'll delve into this challenging topic: ***In the meantime*, what do we do when there's nothing we can do?**

SESSION 1

[THE NEW NORMAL]

We're going to do something a little different in this study. We're going to begin at the end. That's because if you're currently in a challenging season of life and there's no solution to the problem—if you're *in an in the meantime* moment—the good news is that you don't have to give up hope. You might be asking yourself, *Does God hear my prayers? Does God know? Does God care? Is God concerned?* The New Testament has an answer.

In this session, we'll get right to the emotional core of the issue. If you're in the middle of an *in the meantime* moment, it's easy to assume one of three things about God:

1. He is absent.
2. He is apathetic.
3. He is angry with you.

When your circumstances are difficult, you imagine God is too busy running the universe to pay attention to your problems. Or maybe he knows what's going on in your life, but he doesn't care. Or maybe you've done something to make him angry, and he's punishing you by not answering your prayers.

God is not absent. He's not apathetic. He's not angry with you. This is true regardless of how you currently feel. In this session, we'll explore and illustrate these truths.

A DIFFICULT TRUTH

We can all be disobedient. We know the right thing to do, but we do the wrong thing because it's easier or it looks like more fun. We're disobedient with our parents, our coaches, and our employers. We're disobedient with just about any authority figure in our lives . . . including God.

In spite of that disobedience, your heavenly Father loves you. You can know that with confidence, thanks to one of the most famous statements, not just in Scripture but in all of history:

> For God so loved the world that he gave his one and only Son, that whoever believes in him shall not perish but have eternal life. John 3:16

John didn't write "for God so loved the Christians" or "for God so loved the good people" or "for God so loved the obedient people." John knew Jesus personally. He followed him around for three years. He listened to him teach and watched him perform miracles. He had personal conversations with him. When he wrote his gospel, he was an old man looking back on his life and his time with Jesus. He was trying to capture the most important things he'd learned. And he wrote, "For God so loved the world."

The reason you can know that God isn't absent, apathetic, or angry in the midst of your challenging circumstances is that he sent his

Son to die on the cross for you. In doing so, he settled once and for all the question of whether he knows your name and is concerned about your life. But Scripture doesn't just say you can trust that God loves you. It *demonstrates* it.

Lazarus and his sisters, Mary and Martha, were three of Jesus' closest friends. In his gospel, John tells an *in the meantime* story about Lazarus:

> Now a man named Lazarus was sick. He was from Bethany, the village of Mary and her sister Martha. (This Mary, whose brother Lazarus now lay sick, was the same one who poured perfume on the Lord and wiped his feet with her hair.) So the sisters sent word to Jesus, "Lord, the one you love is sick."
>
> When he heard this, Jesus said, "This sickness will not end in death. No, it is for God's glory so that God's Son may be glorified through it." Now Jesus loved Martha and her sister and Lazarus. So when he heard that Lazarus was sick, he stayed where he was two more days, and then he said to his disciples, "Let us go back to Judea."
> John 11:1–7

What would you expect Jesus to do when he finds out someone he loves is sick? He healed all kinds of people that didn't know him personally. But he knew Lazarus. He was friends with Lazarus. He loved Lazarus. So, when he heard that Lazarus was sick . . . he stayed where he was.

When his disciples asked him why he wasn't going to Lazarus right away, Jesus was mysterious. He was up to something they didn't understand. He knew that Lazarus and his sisters would suffer in the short-term. He knew they'd be angry with him. But he also knew that God was about to do something no one anticipated.

Jesus knew Lazarus' name. Don't confuse God's apparent absence for apathy. Jesus loved Lazarus. Don't confuse God's apparent absence for anger at you. On the surface, this isn't a happy message, but it's true and it can offer comfort. You and Lazarus have something in common: your unanswered prayers don't mean God isn't interested.

NOTES Jan 31, 2016

What to do when there is nothing you can do?

New normal - current reality

In the meantime
- I'll never be happy again
- Nothing good can come of this
- No point in continuing

Not true

Important??

Does God Know? Care?

Where is God?

In meantime...

God is not absent, apathetic, or angry.

God's silence does not mean God is absent.

You are not alone & God is not silent.

Dont confuse Gods aparent absence for apathy.

Because of story of John Baptist & Lazarus

true

I can be happy!

Something good can come from this. There's a purpose to this pain!

DISCUSSION QUESTIONS

1. Talk about a season of life—childhood, teenage years, college, early adulthood—that you look back on fondly. What did you enjoy about that season?

2. Have you ever seen someone demonstrate great faith in God despite difficult circumstances? If so, how did that person's faith influence your own?

3. When have you faced a difficult event or season of life that caused you to feel that you'd never be happy again or that no good could come from what you were experiencing? What happened?

4. During the message, Andy asserted that God loves you regardless of whether it feels like he loves you. How would your life be different if you lived as though you fully believed that truth?

5. Talk about a time when you felt God was absent from your life, apathetic about what you were going through, or angry with you. How did it influence your relationship with him? What did you do?

6. If you're ever in the middle of difficult circumstances, what are some practical things you could do to remind yourself that God hasn't abandoned you? What role can a Community Group play in shoring up your faith when God is silent?

THINK ABOUT IT

When we're living *in the meantime*, we're tempted to tell ourselves three lies:

1. "I'll never be happy again."
2. "Nothing good can come from this."
3. "There's no point in continuing."

Those lies strip us of our joy, our hope, and our sense of purpose. But you can restore your joy. You can regain your hope. You can rediscover your sense of purpose. If you are facing this kind of trial right now, you need to renew your mind and remind yourself what is true of you and true of your Father in heaven. You can be happy again.

Something good can come from this. You don't have to be able to see it. You don't even have to be able to imagine it. There's a purpose to this pain.

BEFORE THE NEXT SESSION

Read pages 19–22 for an overview of next session's content.

SESSION 2

[A PURPOSE AND A PROMISE]

When life goes bad, there's something in us that wonders, *God, where are you? What are you doing? Why aren't you fixing this?* We want our pain to go away immediately, and we know God is capable of making that happen. So, why doesn't he intervene?

It may feel like God is absent, apathetic, or angry with us, but there's a difference between our emotions and the truth. In fact, there's no correlation between God's apparent lack of cooperation and his love for us. There's also no correlation between God's apparent lack of cooperation and his existence.

If you are tempted to conclude that God doesn't exist because he won't cooperate, then you must also have been tempted to assume your parents didn't exist because they frequently didn't cooperate. If cooperation were evidence of a person's existence, many people in our lives would not exist.

The idea that God should immediately intervene in our problems is a Western way of thinking. We think we deserve carefree lives. We think things should work out. We assume that's how life is supposed to happen.

Social media only reinforces that notion. We're aware of how well everything seems to be going for everyone else in the world. We don't simply know what's going on in our neighborhoods; we know what's going on in the upscale neighborhoods. We don't simply know what kind of car we drive; we know what kind of car everyone else drives. We don't simply know where our kids go to school; we know where everyone else's kids go to school. We have a perspective that previous generations didn't have. We can compare ourselves not only to the people we see, but to people across our nation and all over the world.

When things don't go well, we immediately throw up our hands and say, "God, why are you leaving me out? There must be something wrong with me!"

But that's not our only option. We can receive our circumstances as a gift with a purpose and a promise.

UNCHANGEABLE CIRCUMSTANCES

The Christian faith was born in difficult circumstances. Jesus' early followers saw him arrested and crucified. They ran for their lives, fearful that they'd be arrested and executed too. Later, after Jesus' resurrection, Christians were persecuted by the Roman Empire. They kept alive the movement Jesus started—at great personal risk and loss. They had a different perspective on suffering than we do. They saw adversity as coming from God.

That radical idea comes from the apostle Paul, who wrote half of the New Testament. In 2 Corinthians, Paul describes his inner turmoil around an affliction that he suffered from and that didn't go away. This affliction made it more difficult for him to do the things that God had called him to do.

> In order to keep me from becoming conceited, I was given a thorn in my flesh, a messenger of Satan, to torment me. Three times I pleaded with the Lord to take it away from me. 2 Corinthians 12:7–8

One of the interesting things about this passage is that when Paul says he was "given a thorn" in his flesh, the Greek word for "given" has a *positive* connotation. It's the most common word used for giving a gift. He didn't consider this affliction a curse or punishment from God. He considered it a gift, given to him by a benevolent, loving God. The phrase "in order that" indicates that there was a purpose behind Paul's affliction. It was meant to keep him from being conceited—from relying too much on his own skills and talents.

When Paul says his affliction was "a messenger of Satan," some people think Satan was literally responsible, and God used what Satan did. Other people think it's a figure of speech (e.g., "It hurt like the devil"). Some people think the affliction was a problem with his eyes. Others think it may have been epilepsy. Whatever Paul's "thorn" was and whatever caused it, two things are clear from the text:

1. Paul saw this thorn as a gift with a purpose.
2. It wasn't going away.

Then the apostle Paul explains what he did when he realized it wasn't going away. The great news for us is that he did what we would do if we found ourselves with something that was painful, humiliating, and debilitating. He says, "Three times I pleaded with the Lord to take it away from me." This indicates there were probably three seasons of his life where this thorn was so unbearable that he finally fell on his knees and said, "God, I cannot continue doing what you've called me to do if you don't remove this."

At some point, you may have been told that the reason your life isn't changing or you're not getting any better is that you don't have enough faith. But the idea that we can "faith" God into something we want him to do is bad theology. The apostle Paul had more faith than all of us put together, and it didn't work for him. He describes how God answered his prayers:

> But he said to me, "My grace is sufficient for you, for my power is made perfect in weakness." Therefore I will boast all the more gladly about my weaknesses, so that Christ's power may rest on me. That is why, for Christ's sake, I delight in weaknesses, in insults, in hardships, in persecutions, in difficulties. For when I am weak, then I am strong. 2 Corinthians 12:9–10

God said no to Paul. But with the no came a promise that God would give Paul strength to live with his affliction and that he would use Paul's weakness to demonstrate his own power.

When faced with challenging circumstances, you have the same option to embrace your weakness and to trust God. Instead of running or hiding from your pain, you can experience Christ's power *through* it. We can experience his grace in a tangible way. Here's why that's important: when you bump up against unchangeable circumstances, your tendency is to hide. That's true of all of us. Our tendency is to pretend. But when you embrace adversity as a gift from God, it transforms the adversity. It gives it a purpose with a promise.

NOTES

View adversity as:
receive adversity as
a gift with a purpose
& a promise!

adversity -
people in Bible knew
adversity they were
use to things being
difficult

Paul said even in
adversity there is the
ability to be content in
Christ.

DISCUSSION QUESTIONS

1. Why do you think people assume that faith in God will remove adversity from their lives? Have you ever made that assumption? If so, how did it influence your relationship with God?

2. Talk about a time when you or someone you knew faced difficult circumstances and God was silent. How did that experience affect your faith in the short-term? How did it affect your faith in the long-term?

3. Is it difficult for you to accept that challenging circumstances can come from the hand of a loving God? Why or why not?

4. Read 2 Corinthians 12:7–10. What would it look like for you to "delight in weakness" for the sake of Jesus? How would it change the way you respond to adversity?

    > In order to keep me from becoming conceited, I was given a thorn in my flesh, a messenger of Satan, to torment me. Three times I pleaded with the Lord to take it away from me. But he said to me, "My grace is sufficient for you, for my power is made perfect in weakness." Therefore I will boast all the more gladly about my weaknesses, so that Christ's power may rest on me. That is why, for Christ's sake, I delight in weaknesses, in insults, in hardships, in persecutions, in difficulties. For when I am weak, then I am strong. 2 Corinthians 12:7–10

5. Do you feel permission to plead with God to take away your difficult circumstances? Do you believe he responds to that kind of prayer? Why or why not?

6. What is the "thorn in your side," the ongoing struggle that you can't change and for which you need to accept God's grace in order to move forward? What can you do to begin to view that "thorn" as a gift that comes with a purpose and a promise from your heavenly Father? How can this group support you?

THINK ABOUT IT

If you've prayed that God would change your circumstances, and you believe that he could if he wanted to but it looks like he isn't going to act on your behalf, you have the option to change your attitude and your perspective about whatever it is you're facing. You have the option to receive your circumstances as a gift with a purpose and a promise. The purpose is yet to be made known. The promise is, "My grace is sufficient for you."

You don't have to view your circumstances as a gift. You have the option to do so. You need to make that choice on your own. God will lead you to the edge of yourself. If you choose to trust him, it will be a revelation, like your eyes have been opened. You will see your circumstances in a whole new light.

BEFORE THE NEXT SESSION

Read pages 27–30 for an overview of next session's content.

SESSION 3

[YES, YOU CAN]

When you think about adversity in your life, it's helpful to remember that the men and women who brought us the New Testament weren't strangers to adversity. In fact, when you read their stories, you realize that conflict was a constant presence in their lives.

Unlike those of us who are Westerners, they didn't see a conflict between the ideas of a good God and adversity in life. The fact that God was good was true even though their lives were full of turmoil and difficulty.

Last week, we explored how the apostle Paul, a man who wrote most of the New Testament and planted churches all along the Mediterranean, struggled with a painful, debilitating, and permanent affliction.

He asked God to remove it. God said no. And Paul continued with the mission to which God had called him. His affliction did not cause him to lose confidence in God. Somehow, he was able to trust God and move on with his life. For him, there was no contradiction between his suffering and God's goodness. Paul was able to live in his *in the meantime* circumstances and still do amazing things . . . things that changed the world . . . things that changed our world.

In this session, we'll explore an incredibly bold statement that Paul made. He assured us that there's a way to find contentment in the midst of incredible adversity. Do you know what contentment means? Contentment is finding inner peace when everything on the outside is going crazy. Contentment is the ability to stop striving internally even as the world around us is out of control.

The apostle Paul said that *in Christ* there is a way to find contentment.

THE SECRET OF CONTENTMENT

About a decade into his mission to plant churches all over the Mediterranean Rim, the apostle Paul was arrested. Eventually, he was held in Rome, awaiting trial. The emperor at that time was Nero, famed for his persecution of Christians. He lit his gardens by covering Christians with tar and lighting them on fire. He publicly blamed Christians for every problem Rome faced. Paul was in a tight spot.

So, here was the apostle Paul, the ambitious go-getter, out of the game and under house arrest. From all appearances, the Roman Empire won, and the kingdom of God lost.

But Paul was ambitious. He had a big vision for changing the world. He decided he wasn't going to waste time and began writing some letters. He wrote letters to the Christian churches in Ephesus, Colossae, and Philippi.

It's important to understand that writing letters was Paul's fallback plan. He only did it because Rome had shut down his mission. There was nothing else he could do. But what he didn't understand was that those letters would change the Western world. They would change the way people viewed God—people that were born centuries after Paul's death. The letters of Ephesians, Colossians, and Philippians, along with others Paul wrote, would become the backbone of the New Testament. Those letters would play a role in bringing the Roman Empire to its knees.

It is in his letter to the Philippians that Paul addresses the issue of contentment. He wrote:

> I know what it is to be in need, and I know what it is to have plenty. I have learned the secret of being content in any and every situation, whether well fed or hungry, whether living in plenty or in want. I can do all this through him who gives me strength. Philippians 4:12–13

You've probably heard this verse or seen it written somewhere. Unfortunately, it's one of the most misapplied verses in the entire Bible. People assume the verse is about accomplishing our goals. Through Christ, we can do anything we set our minds to, right? That's not what Paul was saying.

Paul said that through Christ we could be fine on the inside, even though the world around us was out of control. We can find strength in Christ's strength. We can survive all things. We can thrive under all circumstances. We can maintain our internal composure, not because we're strong, but because Jesus gives us his strength.

That sense of contentment *through Christ* allowed the apostle Paul to remain faithful when remaining faithful was difficult. He had no idea what hung in the balance of that decision. He had no idea what hung in the balance of his decision to continue to follow Jesus when the circumstances pointed against it. He had no idea what God was planning to do through him.

Do you know what hung in the balance? We hung in the balance. The church hung in the balance. Paul accomplished what he did because of his adversity and his response to that adversity.

That's a big deal because you have no idea what or who hangs in the balance of your decision to remain faithful when everything around you says, "Be faithless." You have no idea what God may be doing through your faithfulness when everything around you says, "There's no point in being ethical. There's no point in telling the truth. There's no point in being obedient to God. There's no point in submitting to God."

You have no idea what hangs in the balance, and you'll never know unless you're willing to remain faithful in the midst of adversity. In fact, it's often within the context of adversity that God does his most amazing work *in* us and *through* us.

NOTES

Remain faithful!
you have NO idea what God
may be doing!

Be content - in the meantime.
secret = of being content
I can do all ~~this~~ —
Him
through Christ
Who gives me HIS strength

I can't
He can
He can through me.

mystery of Christ
through you!
creates contentment

DISCUSSION QUESTIONS

1. Do you know someone who lives with pervasive discontentment? If so, how does that discontentment affect the quality of his or her life?

2. Read Philippians 4:10–13. Does the kind of contentment the apostle Paul describes seem achievable in your own life? Why or why not?

3. Why do you think God would use adversity in our lives rather than make the adversity go away?

4. What are some things that make it difficult for you to believe God may do extraordinary and unexpected things through your challenging circumstances?

5. How would your current season look different if you were able to resist the forces, pressures, and temptations of your circumstances?

6. What is your primary source of discontentment right now? What is one thing you can do to live with more contentment out of the knowledge that you can't change your circumstances, but Jesus can? How can this group support you?

THINK ABOUT IT

You can't, but Jesus can. You can be confident that he can because he dragged his own cross to a hill and died for your sin. Anyone who can do that on purpose can strengthen you when you're at your weakest. You can do all things through Christ who strengthens you.

Pray this prayer:

> *"God: I can't; you can. Teach me the mystery of Christ in me."*

BEFORE THE NEXT SESSION

Read pages 35–38 for an overview of next session's content.

SESSION 4

WHERE'S YOUR FOCUS?

When we see bad things happen to good people, it stirs something inside of us. We think it isn't fair. It shakes some of our closely held assumptions about how the world works . . . or at least how it *should* work. Good people should be rewarded with good lives. Only bad people should suffer, right?

But that's not how the world works.

When our own lives blow up, we tend to switch into problem-solving or damage-control mode. We begin to ask questions. That's perfectly normal. We want to know why. We want to know who to blame. We want to know how long the adversity will last. We want to know what the outcome will be.

We ask questions like, "God, are you mad at me?" or "God, are you punishing me?" or "God, did I do something to deserve this?" Throughout history, people have faced tragedy. They have seen bad things happen, and they've asked big questions about those tragedies. Even Jesus' closest followers did this.

This session, we'll look at a conversation that Jesus had with some of his followers. The disciples had some big questions about the suffering they witnessed. But their questions aren't as important as what Jesus had to say.

His response has the power to change the way we see *in the meantime.*

THE BLAME GAME

The gospel of John describes a time when Jesus was walking with his disciples:

> As he went along, he saw a man blind from birth. His disciples asked him, "Rabbi, who sinned, this man or his parents, that he was born blind?" John 9:1–2

Who sinned? Who did it? Who is to blame? Why is this happening? That's what his disciples wanted to know. They're focusing on what went wrong. That's perfectly normal. It's exactly what we do when something goes wrong. "Rabbi, who sinned, this man or his parents, that he was born blind?"

Jesus was faced with this important question. And his answer is fascinating. Jesus didn't say it was the man's fault. Jesus didn't say it was his parents' fault. He didn't point at God's absence, apathy, or anger.

Jesus' answer to this question the disciples asked—a question we often ask—has the power to change our lives. This is what he said:

> "Neither this man nor his parents sinned," said Jesus, "but this happened so that the works of God might be displayed in him." John 9:3

Jesus understood why the disciples were asking the question. But he let them know they were focused on the wrong thing. They wanted to point the finger, but pointing the finger never fixes anything. According to Jesus, the man was born blind "so that the works of God might be displayed in him" *in the meantime.*

Jesus goes on to perform a miracle. He heals the man of his blindness. But the point of the story is not the miracle. Because if the point of the story is the miracle, then what do we do with our afflictions when God doesn't offer any miracles? The point of the story is the conversation that happens before the miracle, when the disciples ask Jesus a question we all have or will have at some point in our lives.

Jesus isn't concerned about who is to blame. He's concerned with God being displayed in the life of the blind man. He's focused on God being on display in the man's circumstances. The same is true of us. When we face challenging circumstances, "whys" and "whose faults" don't matter as much as how God is displayed in our lives.

It's possible that God is on display during our *in the meantime* seasons, and we don't see him. God may be doing something incredible for you, but you don't know it's happening. Hindsight is 20/20. Whenever something difficult is happening or you're in over your head, it's difficult to see anything good coming from the situation. All you can focus on is the fear or the pain right in front of you. But once you have some distance from the situation, your perspective changes. You're able to look back and see the situation more clearly. You can see God on display. And he gives the situation a purpose and a promise.

Don't miss that.

When you focus on what's wrong, you lose sight of what God makes right. You lose sight of what God is doing in your midst, in your circumstances.

NOTES

DISCUSSION QUESTIONS

1. Is it easier for you to connect with God when your circumstances are good or when they're bad? Why?

2. Why is it so tempting for people in the midst of difficult circumstances to compare their lives to the lives of others? What are some of the downsides of making those comparisons?

3. Read John 9:1–3. Have you ever treated a person like a problem to be solved? Explain.

   As he went along, he saw a man blind from birth. His disciples asked him, "Rabbi, who sinned, this man or his parents, that he was born blind? Neither this man nor his parents sinned," said Jesus, "but this happened so that the works of God might be displayed in him." John 9:1-3

4. Talk about a time when you've asked, "Why is this happening to me?" What did you do to manage the circumstances that caused you to ask that question? What was the result?

5. During the message, Andy Jones said, "When you focus on what's wrong, you lose sight of what God makes right." Respond to that statement. Based on your own experiences, does it seem true? Why or why not?

6. As you consider your current circumstances, what is one thing you can do to begin to focus less on what is going wrong and more on what God is making right? What can this group do to support you?

THINK ABOUT IT

As long as you're focused on what went wrong, you're losing sight. You're unable to see what God is making right.

When you realize that, it will change everything. It'll change your heart. It'll change your attitude. It'll change the way you see in the meantime. You'll begin to see that God has been on display all along. You just didn't realize it.

BEFORE THE NEXT SESSION

Read pages 43–46 for an overview of next session's content.

SESSION 5

BELIEVE IT OR NOT

Trials test our confidence in God. They make us wonder if he loves us, is angry with us, or even knows we exist. They make us wonder if he's there at all. But the writers of the New Testament see trials in a different light—not as things that separate us from God, but as things that can connect us to him more deeply.

Jesus said something so audacious and counterintuitive that it's almost offensive. He told us not to worry. Why is that offensive? Consider the trials and adversities people face every day. Maybe you're in the middle of a struggle right now. Some people have incurable illnesses. Others have lost loved ones, and their worlds have been turned upside down. Still others face crushing financial or career challenges. "Don't worry" sounds like an empty and insufficient piece of advice. It's not exactly helpful. If you met someone who was in the middle of tough circumstances, you probably wouldn't tell him or her, "Hey, don't worry."

But Jesus said just that. He said, "Therefore do not worry about tomorrow, for tomorrow will worry about itself. Each day has enough trouble of its own" (Matthew 6:34). Taken out of context, Jesus' words aren't encouraging. We can't just decide to quit worrying . . . can we?

As we near the end of this study, we will explore a single word that is the secret to letting go of worry. It's a word the New Testament authors and Jesus in particular emphasized repeatedly. It's a critical word when we find ourselves in an *in the meantime* set of circumstances.

The word is "believe."

But we're not talking about "believe" as a vague idea or general concept. We're supposed to believe something specific. We're commanded to believe this because intuitively we don't believe it. We're commanded to believe it because, left to our own devices, we would believe the opposite.

But beginning with Jesus and continuing with the apostles, we're told again and again that when we're in an *in the meantime* season and it seems like this is our new reality, there's a big idea we need to embrace and believe.

PERSERVERING FAITH

James was the brother of Jesus. He wrote a letter primarily to Jewish believers in the first century. And that letter ended up in the New Testament. It's full of wisdom and big, challenging ideas. He began his letter like this:

> Consider it pure joy, my brothers and sisters, whenever you face trials of many kinds, because you know that the testing of your faith produces perseverance.
> James 1:2–3

When we face trials, our natural instinct is to dig in our heels and resist. We want to fight hardship or change it. But James urges us to embrace a different mindset. He challenges us to consider trials a source of something good. We don't want to do that. We certainly wouldn't ask other people to do it. It sounds unreasonable.

Our trials put God on trial. They test our confidence in him. They cause us to question his love for us. They cause us to question his presence in our lives. James acknowledges that truth but then points us in a different direction: the testing of our faith has the power to produce a stronger, healthier faith—a *persevering* faith. But only if we choose to embrace a different mindset.

Surprise, undeserved, unavoidable trials are not aberrations. They are expectations. For men and women of faith, they can serve a purpose. They can be beneficial . . . if we allow them to be. In fact, they can be so beneficial that James urges us to be glad. God can and will redeem and use the undeserved, unavoidable, circumstantial trials in our lives.

God honors and is most glorified by persevering faith. The kind of faith that always gets a yes from God doesn't impress anyone. It comes across as magical thinking that has no connection to the challenging world in which we live. The faith that most impresses us is the faith that gets a no from God, or gets no answer from God, and continues to endure.

If it were as simple as praying on Thursday and getting a yes from God by Friday, faith would be about loving a formula, not loving God.

James continued:

> Let perseverance finish its work so that you may be mature and complete, not lacking anything. If any of you lacks wisdom, you should ask God, who gives generously to all without finding fault, and it will be given to you.
> James 1:4–5

What is God up to in the midst of your trials and adversity? James says that God is up to developing persevering faith in you. You may want persevering faith, but you don't want to have to endure the suffering it takes to develop it. But persevering faith is most honoring to God.

Trials produce persevering faith, so James urges us to be patient in our trials—to "let perseverance finish its work." God is at work in your trials. You can hit the eject button, the divorce button, the bankruptcy button, the cheat button, the run button, or the lie button to relieve your pain. But that's robbing yourself of something greater: a persevering faith that is the source of a deeper love of God.

Think about the greatest tension in your life right now. It may be with your spouse or one of your children. It may be financial or professional. It may be with your health. That tension can be the focal point of God's activity in your life . . . if you choose to trust him and allow perseverance to finish its work.

NOTES

DISCUSSION QUESTIONS

1. How do you usually handle sudden changes in your schedule? Do you go with the flow, or does the unexpected stress you out?

2. Talk about a time in your own life or the life of someone you know when good eventually came from adversity. How did that event influence your faith?

3. During the message, Andy said, "Faith that gets a yes from God is nothing compared to faith that gets no answer or no for an answer but endures anyway." How does that statement challenge what you believe (or want to believe) about faith? What is comforting about that statement?

4. Read James 1:2-5. Do you think it's realistic to be able to consider your trials "pure joy"? Why or why not? How would a perspective like that change your relationship with God? How might it change the way you deal with your circumstances?

   > Consider it pure joy, my brothers and sisters, whenever you face trials of many kinds, because you know that the testing of your faith produces perseverance. Let perseverance finish its work so that you may be mature and complete, not lacking anything. If any of you lacks wisdom, you should ask God, who gives generously to all without finding fault, and it will be given to you. James 1:2–5

5. Do you agree with the idea that spiritual maturity has less to do with what you know and more with how you trust God and persevere in the face of adversity? Why or why not?

6. As you think about the adversity you currently face, what is one thing you can do to "let perseverance finish its work"? If you choose to "endure to mature," how might your current circumstances grow your faith? What can this group do to support you?

THINK ABOUT IT

How do you become a mature Christian? You allow perseverance to finish its work. That's simple to understand but difficult to do because it requires that you choose to view your trials in a new way. When you're living *in the meantime*, believe that God is at work in you to mature you. We are perfected through perseverance.

When you're struggling, pray this prayer:

> *"Heavenly Father: I believe you will use this until you choose to remove this. Grant me wisdom to see as you see and strength to do as you say."*

BEFORE THE NEXT SESSION

Read pages 51–55 for an overview of next session's content.

SESSION 6

[COMFORT ZONE]

We don't think of suffering as a positive thing, but it actually has the power to connect us with others. There exists what we might call *a fellowship of suffering*. It's a natural, automatic bond between those who have suffered similarly. When you and another person have suffered similarly, you have a bond. You don't even have to know that person's name. He or she doesn't have to know your name. The bond is there. It transcends education, spiritual knowledge, theology, nationality, and even culture.

Another important thing about the *fellowship of suffering* is that those who have suffered are uniquely qualified to comfort those who are suffering. We've all seen this. Those who have lived through *in the meantime* moments are able to comfort those who are suffering. Those who haven't lived through *in the meantime* moments can offer little help beyond platitudes and empty promises. They can't relate. But when someone who's been there walks into the room to comfort someone who is still there, something powerful happens. It's beyond theology, pastoring, friendship, or good advice.

The *fellowship of suffering* is also vital because comfort from those who have been comforted is life-giving to those who need comfort. It's not just sympathy. It's not just empathy. It is life-giving.

But the most surprising thing about the *fellowship of suffering* is that comforting is life-giving to the comforter as well. When you've journeyed through a deep, dark place and you have the opportunity to come alongside someone facing what you faced, you find life. In that moment, that thing you would never have chosen for yourself and you would never wish upon anybody else suddenly has purpose.

It's an "aha" moment. It's a realization that God really can redeem your suffering. He really can—and does—make something good out of the bad things that happen to you. A pastor can say a prayer for or share a Bible verse with the person who is suffering. But you can connect on a deeper level, offering true comfort. That's because your *in the meantime* moments have given you the credibility and authority that only come from life experiences. And as you comfort the other person, your connection with God grows stronger because you realize he can be trusted with everything that happens in your life, good and bad.

Suddenly, you have a better understanding of the purpose of pain and suffering.

THE GOD OF ALL COMFORT

If we're going to make the most of *in the meantime* moments, we need to understand the role of comfort in our lives. Comfort is an important part of the answer to the question, "What do you do when there's nothing you can do?" In his second letter to the first-century church in Corinth, the apostle Paul addresses the issue of comfort head-on:

> Praise be to the God and Father of our Lord Jesus Christ, the Father of compassion and the God of all comfort.
> 2 Corinthians 1:3

Paul declares God the "Father of compassion" and "the God of all comfort," but that can be difficult to believe when we're suffering. We want to know why he allows bad things to happen. But Paul doesn't hesitate to open that can of worms. He boldly asserts that God is our ultimate source of compassion and comfort. The good news is that Paul wasn't deluded. He didn't live a sheltered life. He didn't have an unrealistic view of how the world works. During his ministry, Paul suffered hardship. His life was continually under threat. He was imprisoned. He was beaten by hostile crowds. He was shipwrecked. He was even bitten by a poisonous snake.

Paul didn't declare God "Father of compassion" and "the God of all comfort" lightly. He understood that God offers a comfort filled with empowering empathy. He offers a comfort that brings courage. He offers a comfort that brings change. God's comfort has the power to steel a person's will to continue. Paul knew that because he'd experienced it himself.

From time to time, we all find ourselves wrestling with the tension between the bad things in the world and a good God. There is a way forward. And we can trust that way because a man who had wrestled with the same tensions brought it to us. Paul's words transcend theology or doctrine. They aren't abstract. They come from having lived the truths he reveals to us. Pain and tragedy don't mean you have to abandon faith in a good and compassionate God.

Paul urges us to pray for comfort in the face of adversity. We rarely do that. We're more inclined to pray that the trouble will go away. We pray for miracles. We pray for change. But Paul says that God is the God of all comfort. That means there's comfort in the circumstances he changes, and there's comfort in the circumstances he chooses not to change. Either way, you can count on the comfort of God. That's a big deal.

Paul goes on to say there's a purpose in our difficult circumstances:

> Praise be to the God and Father of our Lord Jesus Christ, the Father of compassion and the God of all comfort, who comforts us in all our troubles, so that we can comfort those in any trouble with the comfort we ourselves receive from God. 2 Corinthians 1:3–4

Paul says that God comforts us in all our troubles so we're able to comfort others. There are times when God won't deliver you from your trouble because he is doing something in you that you will be able to pass along to other people.

And that's just the beginning. God often comforts us through others so he can later comfort others through us. That's how this works. Regardless of what you're going through, the God of all comfort comforts us in order to equip us.

Paul continues:

> For just as we share abundantly in the sufferings of Christ, so also our comfort abounds through Christ.
> 2 Corinthians 1:5

The phrase "sufferings of Christ" doesn't only refer to the crucifixion. Most theologians agree that Christ suffered just by becoming human. "Sufferings of Christ" means everything he suffered while living on earth. He was hot, cold, lonely, left out, abandoned, and betrayed. He worried about the future as much as the Son of God could worry about anything. He faced a dark night with something ahead of him that he wished he could avoid. And Paul says that just as we share in his suffering, we find comfort in him and through him. In Christ, we are eyeball-to-eyeball with someone who's been there. We can be confident that God knows what human suffering is like.

Paul continues:

> If we are distressed, it is for your comfort and salvation; if we are comforted, it is for your comfort, which produces in you patient endurance of the same sufferings we suffer. And our hope for you is firm, because we know that just as you share in our sufferings, so also you share in our comfort. 2 Corinthians 1:6–7

The reason we receive comfort from God is not simply so we'll be comfortable. It's so we can let others know they can find comfort too. We have the chance to be eyewitnesses to the power of God's comfort.

NOTES

DISCUSSION QUESTIONS

1. Do you tend to learn from the wisdom of others or from your own mistakes? How has that tendency increased or decreased suffering and adversity in your life?

2. Talk about a time when someone who had experienced circumstances similar to yours comforted you. How did you benefit from that person's perspective?

3. Read 2 Corinthians 1:3–7. What is the connection between praising God in the midst of suffering and being able to comfort others? Does that sound too good to be true? Why or why not?

   > Praise be to the God and Father of our Lord Jesus Christ, the Father of compassion and the God of all comfort, who comforts us in all our troubles, so that we can comfort those in any trouble with the comfort we ourselves receive from God. 2 Corinthians 1:3-4

4. Have you ever had the opportunity to comfort someone because you'd experienced something similar to what he or she was going through? If so, how was that experience life-giving for that person? How was it life-giving for you?

5. During the message, Andy said, "Our capacity to comfort is determined by the degree to which we've suffered." Respond to that statement. In what ways is it hopeful? In what ways is it scary?

6. What can you do to begin to receive your adversity as a gift from God and leverage that gift to comfort others? How can this group help you and support you as you take a next step?

THINK ABOUT IT

Make the most of your *in the meantime* moments. Comfort those who need comforting with the comfort you have received from God. Don't bury your sorrows. Leverage them for the sake of other people that you are uniquely qualified to comfort because you've been there, you understand, and you know there's life on the other side.